The War Myth in United States History

C. H. Hamlin

Alpha Editions

This edition published in 2024

ISBN 9789364735872

Design and Setting By
Alpha Editions
www.alphaedis.com
Email - info@alphaedis.com

As per information held with us this book is in Public Domain.
This book is a reproduction of an important historical work.
Alpha Editions uses the best technology to reproduce historical work
in the same manner it was first published to preserve its original nature.
Any marks or number seen are left intentionally to preserve.

Contents

INTRODUCTION	- 1 -
CHAPTER I PATRIOTISM AND PEACE	- 4 -
CHAPTER II THE REVOLUTIONARY WAR	- 6 -
CHAPTER III THE WAR OF 1812	- 15 -
CHAPTER IV THE WAR WITH MEXICO	- 22 -
CHAPTER V THE CIVIL WAR	- 25 -
CHAPTER VI THE WAR WITH SPAIN	- 32 -
CHAPTER VII THE WORLD WAR	- 40 -

INTRODUCTION

Professor Hamlin's book seems to me not merely interesting but extremely important. No man who cares for the story of his country can afford to neglect it.

The plan of the work is suggested by the title;—the time has come to ask soberly regarding every war in which the United States has been engaged from the beginning, whether it had to be, and if it had to be, why? We want to know frankly if our wars have brought us glory. It is already easy to see that the wars of other nations, and especially of those who have fought against us, have entailed upon them shame, cruel measures, oppression of the poor, suppression of liberties, violation of law, destruction of wealth and immeasurable futility. But we were told that our wars had been different; our wars had been sacred; our sovereignty "could do no wrong." Had we not solemnly thanked God for his help in winning every one of our wars?

The great World War has brought mankind to a new and surprising conclusion such as probably never before prevailed at the end of a war. Leading people in all nations are at one in the conclusion, that no thoughtful person in any country which entered the war knew of any adequate reason why his government should spend the blood of its people. As Mr. Lloyd George has said: "No one intended the war, but we all 'staggered and stumbled' into it." It came upon the world like an epidemic of mania. It is evident also that its coming was directly related to the prevailing fashion of "preparedness" for war and to the fears and suspiciousness that everywhere attended this preparedness. It had been the barbarous expectation for ages that war must come every once in so often, as a plague comes. Was not the world full of barbarous people, and therefore of barbarous nations?

Professor Hamlin boldly carries over all the wars of our own United States into the broad generalization which includes the wars of other nations. They all belong together among the old world evils, like slavery or witchcraft, which it is our business to clear away from the earth. We apologize for them no longer. We propose not to expect them nor prepare at tremendous expense to suffer and die when they come; we propose rather through simple, humane and rational measures to provide never to endure them again.

Professor Hamlin accordingly takes up in a rapid survey and analysis each one of the six major wars through which the larger part of our total national expenditures have been devoured. He proceeds, like a skilful surgeon, without passion or partisanship, with a trace of sympathy for all groups and parties, in so far as all were alike victims of misunderstanding, ignorance of the facts, and hereditary prejudices and delusions. Save for the great common human characteristics which gleam out among all peoples and on both sides in times of calamity—the patience, the heroism, the self-sacrifice, the exceptional acts of magnanimity—he finds nothing whatever holy in a single one of our national wars, but rather the manifestation of every mean, cruel and cowardly trait which has ever debased human nature.

He can discover in the case of no one of these wars any evidence that the body of the people or an intelligently informed majority in it, or even the government, had taken pains to assure themselves either of the justice or the necessity of going to war, or that their leaders were ever able to assign a just and sufficient reason and purpose compelling them to resort to war. Thus he brings to light, what every one ought by this time to know, that the Revolutionary War, far from being undertaken by the will of a free citizenry, was actually forced upon the American people by a small minority in the teeth of the earnest opposition of a highly respectable percentage of thoughtful citizens, while another large part of the colonists was quite indifferent to the issue. Professor Hamlin also makes clear that in all our wars, exactly as in those we usually reprobate, our people were presently found practising the same injustices, indignities, lying defamations, detestable acts of revenge, outrages on innocent women and children, upon the fears of which we had hastily assumed excuse for ourselves in rushing into war.

In all our wars we have boasted of our American ardor for liberty. Professor Hamlin's book shows how every great war requires the most terrible form of slavery, namely conscription, in which the individual is stripped of the normal use of his conscience and judgment. In order to drive men to submit to this degradation the government itself, even in the hands of its "best" men, must resort to the employment of unscrupulous lying, reckless propaganda in abuse of the enemy, and the suppression of truth, of free speech and open-mindedness—in short, to a debauch of miseducation, and a general corruption of the whole population. Once in war, it never will do to let good be known of the enemy! War counts upon the plentiful outpouring of passion and hatred.

The churches also are pressed in war-time to undertake the defense of doing evil that good may come, and to strain their arguments over the verge of hypocrisy in making the worse appear the better reason. So altogether, "hell is let loose." The worst of it is that the lower passions, once let loose, do not willingly return under control, but remain to haunt the earth.

Once more, Professor Hamlin shows how in each case after a war the whole horrible storm flattens out into waste, corruption and futility. The World War is the most colossal demonstration of this condition. If a people thought they knew what they were fighting for, they failed to get it; the victor proves often at last to be the vanquished. It is curious now in looking back to the Civil War to note that the reason which chiefly persuaded "good" and chivalrous souls to engage in it was to put an end to slavery. This at best was dealing in the wrong way with evil, that is, overcoming it with evil, as was abundantly proved after the war. But Mr. Lincoln would not admit that we were at war against slavery! We were at war, as the government held, to put down secession, whereas we had begun the national union by a war of secession; our government would have liked at the time of the war of 1812 to get Canada by secession or capture; we fought with Mexico to secure the results of the secession of Texas; we refused in 1898 to accept a peaceful method to separate Cuba from Spain but insisted upon fighting to effect the separation; and we still keep armed forces in the Philippine Islands against the protest of the inhabitants. Mr. Roosevelt was quick to postulate the right of secession in the case of Panama. As to the Great War, our President Wilson's proclamation in favor of the natural right of small nations to secede has become one of the slogans of mankind! As has been often remarked: "This is a queer world." Professor Hamlin's little book is at least an easy *reductio ad absurdum* for war.

CHARLES F. DOLE.

Southwest Harbor, Me.,
August, 1926.

CHAPTER I

PATRIOTISM AND PEACE

For the first one hundred and thirty-five years of the history of this republic the total expenditure of the federal treasury was approximately $66,000,000,000. Of this total expenditure approximately $56,000,000,000 was for warfare. From 1775 to 1923 the United States Army was engaged in no conflicts comprising about 8,600 battles and a casualty list of approximately 1,280,000 men. (See Ganoe, History of U. S. Army, page 490.) Of course most of these conflicts were minor. This study will include only the six major wars in which we have been participants.

A most common fallacy in the study of history is the blind acceptance of that which has happened as inevitable in the course of events. This is a form of collective fatalism. It reduces history to a study of the dead past with no message for today. This view is the very opposite of democracy. Democracy assumes that the group has control over its actions and that they are not the result of a blind fatalism. To look upon past events as inevitable makes man the victim of forces over which he can have no control. It makes man a slave. This fatalism is incompatible with democracy. The democrat must study history not to discover the forces of fate but to discover more perfect rules of human conduct. Primarily, the study of the past should be to throw light on the present and future, so that we might profit by the wisdom and the mistakes of the past. But to do this we can not accept collective fatalism as our attitude toward history.

Until the beginning of the nineteenth century the study of history was a study of the Greeks and the Romans. It was a study of the ancients only. Early in the nineteenth century, with the rise of nationalism especially intensified by the French Revolution, all nations began introducing the study of their national history in their elementary schools. The object of this was to teach patriotism. Examine their meaning of patriotism and you find it meant the support of the king on the throne. All texts and instruction exalted the nation to show its superiority to others. Patriotism meant national propaganda. With the rise of democracy patriotism began to shift to mean the support of the group,—pro-group rather than pro-king. This was the cause and the result of the national mind set. Patriotism became international hatred, measured in terms of military service. This attitude toward history caused the teaching and writing of history to be

- 4 -

largely national propaganda, by interpreting all the wars of a nation as defensive with the opponent always the offensive nation.

The greatest difference between the present peace movement and previous ones is that now among many of those who study the problem the offensive-defensive relationship in warfare is being not only questioned but rejected. All nations picture their side as defensive. Previous peace movements accepted this attitude. Accordingly, when a conflict arose, these opponents of war usually yielded to the pressure because they thought their nation was being attacked by an aggressor. But a careful study of history does not warrant such an idea. The effective element of the present peace movement is based chiefly on the fact that there is no nation of "sole guilt" in any war once the facts are studied carefully. The following study is an attempt to show that in our wars there has not been the "sole innocence" of the United States as opposed to the "sole guilt" of our opponents. *That its wars are defensive against an offensive enemy, is the war myth of every country.* This national bias makes it easy for the military party to predominate and to precipitate war. Yet warfare is not popular if measured in terms of voluntary support of the citizenship in time of war. It was hard for the colonies to induce as many as 250,000 men to join the Revolutionary forces out of a total population of over 3,000,000, and only a part of the 250,000 were enlisted at any one time. In the Civil War both sides were forced to use the draft, or the war would have collapsed. No major war of modern times could have been fought without the draft. This would be enough to show that warfare is not popular if judged by actual voluntary support on the field of battle.

One often hears that warfare is a manifestation of human nature and will be eliminated only through a long evolutionary process. But the same thing has been said of slavery, duelling, witchcraft, and many other evils now eliminated. Warfare is not dependent upon human nature, but upon the human point of view, and this point of view can be altered by education,—education which is honest, which can sift the true from the false, which does not close its eyes to the powerful role played by economic and social forces in the wars of the nation.

Whether there was another way out in these conflicts, whether the results aimed at were achieved, whether the ruin and destruction which went hand in hand with these conflicts could ever be balanced by material acquisitions,—these are questions the reader must decide for himself. This book simply lays the facts before him.

CHAPTER II

THE REVOLUTIONARY WAR

In no sense is an attempt being made here to give a complete history of the causes of the war for the independence of the United States. This is simply a brief analysis of the ten outstanding causes and the nature of the conflict, without defending or opposing either side in the struggle.

The common opinion in the United States regarding the American Revolution is that it was a war waged against Great Britain in which the American people as a whole rose up against the mother country in order to protect themselves against unjustifiable and unbearable oppression. This is the position taken in the Declaration of Independence, and we have always looked upon the conflict through the eyes of the Declaration of Independence. The thirteen colonies declared themselves free and independent on July 2, 1776, and then on July 4, 1776 adopted the Declaration of Independence proclaiming to the world their reasons for declaring themselves free. Thus the Declaration of Independence was not a declaration of independence, but a publication to the world of the causes which led the colonies to the point of such a declaration. It was an effort to put their side before the world and justify it. It was written by Thomas Jefferson in the heat of a great emotion. Twenty-seven grievances were held against Great Britain to justify the course taken by the colonies. We shall not attempt here to study the real nature of "freedom" which is much more than a question of national boundaries, and is even independent of national boundaries,—but we shall accept the term in its usual narrow legal sense.

The outstanding causes of the Revolutionary War were the following: the expulsion of the French from Canada in 1763, the attempt on the part of Great Britain to enforce the navigation acts, the British western land policy, the British financial legislation regarding the colonies, the stamp act of 1765, the Townshend act of 1767, the Boston "tea party" of 1773, the five punitive acts of 1776, the general economic depression during the 70's, and religious conflicts. Let us examine briefly these ten causes.

(1) After the French were defeated by Great Britain in 1763 and lost Canada, the colonies did not feel the same need for protection by the mother country as formerly. The French on the north were defeated. The Indians gave some trouble but were not a great power to be dreaded. As a result, the colonies felt themselves to be self supporting. Georgia was an exception because as the youngest of the thirteen colonies it was dependent

on England for subsidies and protection from the Indians. Thus, because the people recognized their dependence on Great Britain for protection, the movement for independence made slower headway in Georgia.

(2) By far the most important cause of the American Revolution was the effort on the part of George III to enforce the navigation laws of Great Britain. It was customary then for every mother-country to regard its colonies as trading posts. The colonies were considered necessary as the source of raw materials for the home manufacturers and also as a market for the surplus manufactured goods of the home country. This economic principle was a phase of mercantilism which was the dominant economic doctrine of the time. In harmony with this theory, Great Britain as early as 1651 began passing navigation acts requiring her colonies to trade only with British merchants. All the export trade of the colonies had to be sent to Great Britain, and all their imported goods had to come from Great Britain. In addition, the ships transporting these goods had to be owned by British subjects.

This law, however, was openly violated by the colonial merchants. They traded with the Dutch or with any other foreigners they could. British officials in America were bribed and co-operated in this illegal trade. The leading people of New England at this time were merchants, and it has been estimated that nine-tenths of these merchants were smugglers. John Hancock, who was to become president of the First Continental Congress in 1775, was a smuggler on a great scale, and at one time was sued for $500,000 as a penalty for smuggling. John Adams was his counsel. (See Simons, "Social Forces in United States History," pages 61-62.) It was these merchants of New England and especially of Boston, who were among the leaders in the Revolution. After the close of the French and Indian War in 1763, English merchants and English business in general had to be heavily taxed in order to pay the enormous national debt. Accordingly, pressure was brought to bear on the British government to have the navigation laws enforced, which would give the English the colonial trade, thus enabling them to meet more easily the financial demands of taxation. Efforts were then made by Great Britain to enforce these navigation laws which had been openly violated for more than a century. Their legality had never been questioned. It was the usual policy of all countries of that age in dealing with their colonies. These navigation laws were no doubt unwise interferences with trade but their legality was not questioned, as all modern tariffs are trade barriers, which does not make their violation legal. Besides, these laws did not entirely disregard the interests of the colonies. Great Britain gave them a monopoly of tobacco raising, prohibiting Ireland from raising it. Bounties or sums of money were often paid by the British Government to the colonial producers to encourage industry. These bounties were paid on indigo, tar, pitch, hemp, and many other industries which Great Britain was attempting to establish in the colonies in order to keep the empire from finding it necessary to buy them from a foreign nation. These navigation laws aroused New England rather than the South, for it was the commercial section of the country.

(3) Another cause of friction between the colonies and the mother country was the British land policy proclaimed in 1763. This policy ordered the colonial governors to grant no more land to settlers beyond a certain western border extending south from the New England States along the western part of New York, Pennsylvania, Virginia, North Carolina, South Carolina, and Georgia. (See Hockett, "Political and Social History of the United States," Vol. 1, page 115.) This line extended down just east of the mountains and was to leave to the Indians the territory west of it. This western land was then to be purchased from the Indians for the king. After that the Indians would go further west and their original territory was to be opened to settlers as soon as it was purchased. This arrangement was made by Great Britain to avoid conflict between the Indians and the frontier settlers. The frontier settlers, however, objected, preferring to drive the Indians back by more ruthless methods even if it caused trouble. The western land speculators also did not like it because they could not sell their land until Great Britain had first pushed the Indians back. The royal government immediately began making treaties with the Indians for the purchase of their territory. The policy was wise and humane but the settlers were too impatient to abide by it. (The Washington family was prominent in these western land speculations.) A land lobby was kept in London by these speculators in their efforts to get large grants of western land from the crown and then to sell it off as the country became more and more settled.

(4) The next principal cause of trouble was the British financial legislation regarding the colonies. The colonies had issued fiat money or colonial bills of credit, which were a form of paper money. These could not be redeemed, and immediately began to depreciate in value. Yet they were made legal tender by the colonial legislature, so that they had to be accepted in payment of debt. Often the colonies would buy goods from the English and pay them with this colonial money. The southern planters were especially active in using it to pay their debts to their British creditors. The merchants of London soon complained of this practice. Finally, in 1764, Great Britain prohibited all the colonies from issuing these bills of credit or fiat money as such a procedure was considered unfair to their creditors. This, of course, aroused great opposition from those profiting by this currency when paying their debts. Yet no one now would defend such a financial policy on the part of the colonies.

- 8 -

(5) The popular conception today is that the Stamp Act of 1765 was the principal if not the sole cause of the American Revolution. This fact is greatly exaggerated but it is the easiest to understand, and for that reason has been given the chief place among the many causes of the conflict. The Stamp Act was an act passed by Great Britain requiring the placing on all legal documents of stamps to be sold to the colonies by Great Britain. The usual impression is that this revenue was to go to the mother country and was to be a continual tax upon the colonies for the sole benefit of the crown. This impression is entirely false, however. The revenue from these stamps was to be used to pay one-third of the expense of a colonial army of about 10,000 men to be kept here for the defense of the colonies. Not one penny was to go to Great Britain. Examine any elementary text on United States history. They speak of taxing the colonies, but leave the impression that the money was to go to Great Britain, whereas actually it was all to be spent for the protection of the colonies against possible trouble with the Indians and the French. This colonial army had been proposed before by the colonies. In 1739 colonial leaders under the leadership of the Governor of Pennsylvania had themselves proposed such an army supported by such a tax. But at that time they had felt the danger of the French in Canada. After the defeat of the French in 1763 this danger was no longer so threatening. When this Stamp Act was passed in 1765 its operation was delayed for one year in order to give the colonies an opportunity to agree among themselves upon some other method of raising the money if they objected to the Stamp Act. The act was repealed in 1766 because of the bitter opposition of the colonies, who disliked a tax of any sort. "No Taxation Without Representation" has been greatly over-emphasized. It is only half true, for it implies that taxation with representation would have been accepted.

(6) When the colonies objected to the Stamp Act, calling it an "internal" tax, Great Britain repealed it and in 1767 passed the Townshend Act, which provided for a tariff on imports to the colonies. The imported goods, however, were boycotted and Great Britain was forced to repeal the tariff on imports in 1770. The amount of imported goods in the New England colonies alone dropped from 1,363,000 pounds in 1768 to 504,000 pounds in 1769. After the repeal in 1770 the imports in 1771 were doubled. Thus the boycott was a powerful weapon in the hands of the colonies. With it the colonies were in a position to enforce almost any demand they liked upon Great Britain.

(7) When the Townshend duties were repealed in 1770 a tax was still left on tea, in order to assert the right to levy such a tax. In 1773, Great Britain allowed a tea company known as the East India Company to bring over a large quantity of tea. This company had been given a monopoly of

- 9 -

the colonial tea market. When this tea arrived in Boston, on December 16, 1773, a group of men entered the ship and threw overboard the cargo valued at about £15,000. But why was this tea destroyed? Simply because the leaders in this act were tea merchants in Boston, whose trade would have to compete with the newly arrived tea had it been permitted to enter the market. The act was the destruction of private property on the part of the participants. The more moderate element in Boston wanted the tea paid for and the action repudiated.

(8) As a punishment for this performance, Great Britain passed the five punitive or coercive acts of 1774. These five acts were the following: Close the port of Boston until the tea should be paid for. Revise the charter of Massachusetts. Send to England for trial colonial agents accused of violence in the execution of their duties. Station soldiers in Massachusetts to aid in the execution of law. Annex to Quebec the land between the Ohio River and the Great Lakes. These acts were all legal. Great Britain had as much right to demand that Boston pay for the tea destroyed as we have to demand that a foreign power compensate our subjects for property lost there through the mob action of its subjects.

(9) Another cause of the Revolution often overlooked was the general economic depression both in Great Britain and the colonies following the close of the French and Indian War in 1763. This was felt in all industries. Depressions of this sort always create political unrest and a desire for change in government, even though the authorities in power are in no way responsible for the condition. This is especially true in American political history. Presidential elections have been determined by economic conditions having no direct bearing upon the issues involved.

(10) The tenth and last cause we shall give of the American Revolution was the religious cause. There was a movement on foot to locate an Episcopal bishop in the colonies. At that time all the clergy of the Episcopal Church were ordained in England as there was no bishop here. Consequently, all the Episcopal ministers came from abroad and they were often mediocre, for the more efficient among them were kept in England. In 1770 there were about two hundred and fifty Episcopal clergy in the colonies, most of whom were in Virginia. The rumor of locating a bishop here aroused resentment in the other denominations who unanimously opposed the plan. But the most effective religious cause of the Revolution came from still another source. When Great Britain extended Quebec down between the Ohio River and the Great Lakes, the Catholic Church was made the established church of these regions, as it was in Quebec. This greatly incensed all Protestants and "no pope no king" became one of the slogans of the Revolution. John Adams considered this religious animosity "as much as any other a cause" of the war for independence. Both these

attitudes on the part of the colonies were unwise. An Episcopal bishop was badly needed here to elevate the Episcopal clergy and remove the unworthy ministers. The prejudice against Catholics was simply folly. The Catholic priests in the colonies unanimously supported the Revolution.

If we examine the acts of Great Britain which brought on the Revolution we find that they were all legal. They were all in harmony with the spirit of the age. There was simply a general breakdown of mercantilism. Patrick Henry especially talked about "rights as British subjects," but there were no such rights of which the colonies were being deprived. Had they remained in England they would have enjoyed no privileges of which they were deprived by coming to America. Talk of this sort made effective oratory, but was false when examined. "No Taxation without Representation" is not a legal matter but commonplace political philosophy. We have many other examples of taxation without representation. The great majority of people in England were then disfranchised yet taxed. Women were taxed before they were given the ballot. Many people are now taxed even in those states where they are deprived of the ballot. Phrases, as this regarding taxation, were merely effective generalities without real meaning. The mistake of Great Britain was not in the passage of any illegal or unusual laws for governing the colonies, but it was in trying to rule a group of people against their will. Such a policy invariably invites trouble.

Instead of thirteen units, as we usually regard the thirteen colonies, there were three units differing in economic and political ideals. The coastal plains extending from New Hampshire to Pennsylvania constituted one, which was dominated by commercial interests. The second was the tidewater section from Maryland to Georgia, which was primarily agricultural and was dominated by the planters. The third unit or section was the frontier with extreme ideas about political democracy. The first unit was commercial and interested in trade and shipbuilding. Great mercantile families had grown up there accumulating their wealth largely through smuggling with the West Indies. To them the navigation laws were especially offensive. Their chief desire was to restore the commercial conditions before 1763, yet they bitterly opposed a withdrawal from the British Empire, for they wanted its protection. They dominated Boston, Newport, New York, and Philadelphia. They were Whig in opposing trade restrictions, but Tory in opposing separation. They had no sympathy with the political radicalism of Jefferson, Henry, and such leaders. The second region was the tidewater region of the South. It was dominated by the planters, many of whom were heavily in debt to British creditors. They secured the passage of lax bankruptcy laws detrimental to non-resident creditors. These laws, however, were vetoed by the king as were the laws providing for colonial bills of credit. These planters felt themselves aristocrats. Although they opposed British financial policy, they likewise objected to the democracy of Jefferson. The third section was the frontier. This section had often been discriminated against by the older sections in matters of representation in the colonial assemblies, administration of justice, and taxation. Its inhabitants were zealous for popular rights and had no economic interests to the contrary. In domestic politics they were out of harmony with the commercial and planter sections. Their zeal for imaginary "rights of man" gave great impetus to the movement for independence. Henry and Jefferson were the leaders of this section and their point of view prevailed when the Declaration of Independence was written, the ideas of which were shocking to the other sections.

These three sections reacted differently to the various British Acts. In Georgia, the frontier people were pro-British because they were dependent upon Great Britain for subsidies and protection from the Indians. The frontier people of North Carolina were also Tory because they had a sharp difference with the eastern part of the state. Had the frontier of all the colonies had a similar sharp difference with the coastal plains they would no doubt have been Tory and defeated the Revolution. The frontier of Virginia got possession of the state and furnished such leaders as Henry and Jefferson.

The Revolution was the American phase of an English civil war. It was not so much a conflict between England and the colonies as between different classes of the English people. It was struggle between liberals and conservatives. The liberals were in control in the colonies while the conservatives were in control in England. In both countries there was a large and influential minority group. The thirteen colonies were a part of the British Empire and simply seceded, as the South did in 1860.

The terms "Whig" and "Tory" are often misleading or vague when applied to this period. Many Whigs of Great Britain, such as Burke, Fox and Pitt, were opposed to the British policy of regulating the colonies, but they were equally opposed to granting them independence. Many of the American moderates were Whig in opposing the British navigation policy, but wanted to pay for the tea destroyed in Boston. Many advocated an imperial union to handle such questions in the future. The radicals were for complete home rule and got control of the First Continental Congress of 1774. There was never a general uprising of the whole colonial population. John Adams estimated that about one-third of the population were opposed to separation. The greatest problem of the Revolutionists was to keep the spirit of revolt alive. About 25,000 Americans enlisted in the British army.

When the radicals declared the colonies independent in 1776 many men of property were shocked—Henry Laurens wept when he heard the Declaration of Independence read—but there was rejoicing among the radicals. A horse-jockey neighbor said to John Adams: "Oh! Mr. Adams, what great things you and your colleagues have done for us! There are no courts of justice now in the Province and I hope there never will be any."

There are many facts regarding our conduct during the Revolution which are not pleasant to relate. For example, on June 1, 1775, Congress passed a resolution disclaiming any intention of invading Canada. The report of this decision was widely circulated in Canada. About four weeks later Congress secretly made plans for the invasion of Canada that fall. The invasion took place in September, 1775, but Canada drove the invaders back. (See Lecky, "The American Revolution," page 215.) Is there any difference between our invasion of Canada and the German invasion of Belgium? Many people suspected of being Tories were terribly badly treated. The New York legislature passed a resolution that Tories should be "deemed guilty of treason and should suffer death." They were often hunted by mobs, tarred and feathered, and killed. American troops set fire to the houses of the people to plunder and rob. In fact in some sections the colonists looked upon the British army with as much favor as the American army. New York alone confiscated $3,600,000 worth of property belonging to Tories, and all the states did likewise. During that entire period the Tories were the great sufferers. It is obvious that a person had as much legal and moral right to be a Tory as to be a Whig, provided he committed no act of violence against society, and the great majority of Tories had committed none. It was simply a question of difference in opinion. To punish a person for a difference of opinion cannot of course be harmonized with democracy,—majority rule does not mean coercion of minorities. Dictatorship of the majority can be the worst kind of despotism. When Great Britain recognized the independence of the colonies in 1783, one provision of the treaty agreed to by both parties was that the Tories should be compensated by the states for the property confiscated during the conflict. The states, however, did nothing about it, but treated that provision as a "scrap of paper."

Was our separation from Great Britain a wise or an unwise step? It is impossible to answer a question of this sort with certainty. We assume that it was wise and beneficial. But to determine that, it would be necessary to roll history back, to let us remain a part of Great Britain, and then compare the two conditions. It has been argued that if we had remained a part of the British Empire the democratic spirit of the colonies would have been a great help to the democratic element in Great Britain, that these elements co-operating would have democratized and federated all the English-speaking peoples, which, in turn, would have aided in democratizing the world. Such an idea cannot be upheld with assurance, but neither can one say dogmatically that the American Revolution resulting in our separation was for the best. We use the terms "freedom" and "independence" in too loose a sense when we say that we then gained our freedom or independence. Would the South have been free and independent if it had been the winning faction in the Civil War? Secession or the changing of national boundaries does not give freedom. Canada is free although a part of the British Commonwealth; Texas is free although a part of the United States.

BIBLIOGRAPHY

Faulkner, Harold Underwood—*American Economic History*, pages 137-139.

Hayes, C. J. H.—*Political and Social History of Modern Europe*. Vol. I, chapter 10.

Hockett, H. C.—*Political and Social History of United States*. Vol. I, chapters 5, 6, 7, 8.

Lecky, E. H.—*The American Revolution*.

Muzzey, D. S.—*The United States of America Through the Civil War*. Vol. I, chapter 2.

Schlesinger, A. M.—*New Viewpoints in American History*. Chapter 7.

Simons, A. M.—*Social Forces in American History*. Chapters 6 and 7.

CHAPTER III

THE WAR OF 1812

There were two different causes of the war with Great Britain in 1812, and it is necessary to examine each separately. These causes were maritime rights and land hunger.

The general European upheaval from 1789 to 1815, known as the French Revolution, soon developed into a war between Great Britain and Napoleon. All Europe was divided into two camps, with Great Britain and Napoleon as the leaders on their respective sides. Almost a decade before 1812 Great Britain began issuing decrees known as Orders in Council. These "Orders in Council," issued in the name of the king, attempted to prohibit neutral nations from shipping goods to France. In this manner, a blockade was proclaimed against France, and ships attempting to get through the lines were subject to capture and confiscation.

Napoleon issued similar decrees, known as the Berlin and Milan Decrees, declaring that any ships en route to Great Britain would be subject to capture, for France had also blockaded Great Britain. But as neither blockade could be fully enforced, they were both to a large degree disregarded. Both Great Britain and Napoleon were attempting to cut off each other's trade and not primarily trying to disregard the rights of neutrals. All goods attempting to run these blockades were subject to capture.

The principal losers through these captures were the New England traders, but they preferred losing occasional ships to joining in a war which would involve them with their principal customer, Great Britain. There had been no serious crisis since 1807, five years before war was declared. Napoleon was then losing fast and it seemed evident that it would be only a short while before the causes of friction would be over. The flagrant disregard of the "rights" of neutral trade had taken place before 1807. In 1812, the solution or end of the problem was in sight. In 1810, our registered tonnage in foreign trade was 981,019 tons, which high mark it was not to reach again till 1847. Our foreign trade was not ruined, and the New England merchants who sustained the loss wanted nothing done. They were Federalists and would have preferred a war with France rather than a war with England, because they regarded Napoleon as the real cause of all the trouble. The Federalists were pro-British, while the Democrat-Republicans were pro-French. Early in 1811 our minister, William Pinkney,

- 15 -

left London, and thus the United States was cut off from a knowledge of the movements in England. England was attempting to avoid war with America because such a war would naturally hurt her foreign trade and domestic prosperity. By the spring of 1812 England was ready to revoke the Orders in Council as soon as it could be done with dignity, but this fact was unknown to America. On June 23, 1812, the orders were revoked. But this was five days after the war of 1812 had been declared. England did not know war was declared when the orders were revoked, and the United States did not know till a good while later in the season that the orders had been revoked. Perhaps modern cable communication would have prevented this war.

Another source of friction lay in the impressment of seamen and sailors. During this period Great Britain was hard pressed for men in her naval campaign against Napoleon. Many sailors deserted English ships and came to America because of the higher wages paid by the owners of American ships. Every British warship anchoring in American waters would lose a good part of its crew, who would secure positions on American ships. Great Britain demanded the return of these deserters, who would often become naturalized citizens. Great Britain, however, at that time regarded citizenship as a contract between citizens and government which could not be broken without the consent of both, disqualifying the sailor from citizenship in the United States, without her consent. This European custom has now disappeared, of course, and one can change citizenship at will.

When the United States refused to return these men, the British ships would search American vessels on the high seas to see if any British sailors were on board. This policy of impressment waned, however, after 1805, because Napoleon had been defeated on the sea and Great Britain was not in such great need of sailors. Impressment was not made a cause of war until after the war had begun and President Madison had learned that the Orders in Council had been revoked. President Madison in 1812 estimated the number of impressments at 6,057, but the Massachusetts legislature appointed a committee to investigate the situation, which reported that the Madison estimate was "three or four times too large." Great Britain took the position that the United States was acting as a harbor for her deserters from the British navy and merchant ships, and that therefore the search was warranted as a defensive measure.

The British "Orders in Council" prohibiting the trading of neutral powers with France, and the British impressment of fugitive sailors from English ships, were the maritime controversies which resulted in the War of 1812. Both policies on the part of Great Britain were adopted as necessary measures in her conflict with Napoleon.

The New England Federalists were the people principally concerned in the United States, but they opposed the war. War was declared by a vote of 79 to 49 in the House, and 19 to 13 in the Senate. There was open discouragement of enlistment in New England. The Governors of Massachusetts and Connecticut refused to honor President Madison's call for the militia. Henry Adams estimated that the New England bankers loaned more money to Great Britain than to the United States for war purposes. Of the $17,000,000 in specie in the country in 1812, about $10,000,000 was in the hands of the New England Federalists. They subscribed less than $3,000,000 to the United States war loan. Thus, strangely, enough, the War of 1812 was fought in spite of the protest of those for whom it was presumably fought.

But in recent years another cause of the war and the chief cause has been discovered. This was land hunger.

The United States entered the conflict at the insistence of the south and west, despite the opposition of the northeastern states. The inland section overruled the opposition of the maritime section. At that time, there was an ardent expansionist sentiment along the whole western and southern border looking towards the annexation of Canada and Florida, with a vaguer idea of seizing all of the Spanish possessions of North America. Spain then owned Florida. Spain and Great Britain were allies against Napoleon, and a war with one was looked upon as a war with both. The belief that the United States would some day annex Canada had existed continuously since the Revolution. Benjamin Franklin had advocated the buying of Canada by the United States, since we failed to take it during the Revolution. The Continental Congress made an effort to capture Canada, but our armies were repulsed. Washington had objected to leaving Canada in British hands. In 1803 Governor Morris of Pennsylvania wrote that at the time of the Constitutional Convention he knew "that all North America must at length be annexed to us—happy indeed if the lust of dominion stop there." This idea, however, was a vague dream till about 1810.

There had been friction in the northwest between the Americans and British. The British retained trading posts in the northwest after they had agreed to give them up by the treaty of 1783 recognizing the independence of the United States. These were held to compensate the Tories for their property confiscated during the Revolutionary War, which had not been done. For this reason, the British held the northwest posts until 1796, when they were given up by the Jay Treaty. All the Indian trouble in that section was attributed to British propaganda, which incited the Indians against the United States. The Canadian traders made friends with the Indians to get their trade while the Americans were aggressively pushing them back from

- 17 -

their land. The result was that the Indian was more friendly to the British in Canada than to the United States.

The idea of annexing Canada was intensified after 1810 because of the belief that the Indians were being turned against the United States by the British. The south was almost unanimous in its demand for the annexation of Florida, while the southwest was taking a lively interest in Mexico. This land hunger was making its appearance rapidly, but it was several years later that the phrase "manifest destiny" was to come into general use.

President Madison and Secretary of State James Monroe were eager to annex Florida. Thomas Jefferson was interested in the annexation of Canada, Florida and Cuba. Jefferson considered the acquisition of Canada only a "question of marching," with Florida and Cuba easy prey from Spain. These expansionists were in favor of declaring war, while the rest of the country opposed the idea.

When Congress met in 1811, Henry Clay was elected Speaker of the House. He was leader of the war group known as "war hawks." Clay was the first Speaker of the House of Representatives to recognize the great power he could exercise over legislation through his appointment of committees. He was the first "Czar" of the House. On the Foreign Relations Committee, Clay appointed Peter B. Porter, Chairman, Calhoun of South Carolina, Grundy of Tennessee, Harper of New Hampshire, and Desha of Kentucky. All these were ardent expansionists and reliable war men. They represented the frontier section of 1812, and Clay had been chosen Speaker by the representatives from that section. In December, 1812, while on the Foreign Relations Committee, Porter said in discussing trouble with Great Britain, "We could deprive her of her extensive provinces lying along our border to the north." Grundy and Rhea, ardent expansionists from Tennessee, agreed.

R. M. Johnson of Kentucky during the same session made the statement, "I shall never die contented until I see her (Great Britain's) expulsion from North America, and her territories incorporated with the United States," and Harper of New Hampshire said in Congress: "To me, sir, it appears that the Author of Nature has marked our limits in the South by the Gulf of Mexico, and in the North by the regions of eternal frost."

These statements were representative of the sentiments of the members in Congress from the western section. The Federalist Party consisted chiefly of the mercantile and financial interests of the coast towns. They were solidly against expansion, which would give the economic advantage to the western section of the country.

The winter of 1811-1812 saw a great expansionist wave sweep over the west, clamoring for the annexation of Canada. Contemporary newspapers were filled with editorials demanding annexation. The cry came up from the whole frontier, New Hampshire to Kentucky, to expel the British from Canada. At a Washington's birthday dinner given at Lexington, Ky., on February 22, 1812, the toast proposed was "Canada and our arms." Although the frontier claimed that the British were inciting the Indians against the United States, L. M. Hacker in "Western Land Hunger and the War of 1812" proves that the Indian menace was greatly exaggerated, but that land hunger was the real motive.

Randolph, of Virginia, who was opposed to the war, said in 1812 on the floor of Congress: "Ever since the report of the Committee on Foreign Relations came into the House, we have heard but one word—like the whippoorwill with but one eternal monotonous tune—Canada! Canada! Canada!"

The south and southwest were interested in the annexation of Florida and possibly Texas. To them, a war with Great Britain meant a war with Spain also, since the British and Spain were then in alliance.

President Madison and Secretary of State Monroe, in their eagerness to acquire Florida, had helped a General George Mathews to instigate a revolution in Florida. In 1812 General Mathews took American troops to Florida, with the co-operation of the War Department and also the support of Governor Mitchell of Georgia. This territory was held for a year, although Congress twice refused to authorize the President to hold it. Finally Madison was forced to repudiate the act because of the opposition of the Federalists and the northern members of his own party. Senator Crawford, of Georgia, was active in his support of southern expansion; Jefferson wished to annex Cuba as a state, and Madison and Monroe were eager to annex Florida although they were not concerned with the appropriation of Canada.

The interest of the southwest in Mexico was a spirited one. McCaleb, in his book on "The Aaron Burr Conspiracy" points out that Burr simply attempted to do in 1806 what the whole southwest was dreaming of. He was conspiring against Spain in Mexico and not against the United States as is usually supposed. "Lands, water-ways, and Indians" was the cry of men desiring to drive out Spain.

In the Nashville *Clarion* of April 28, 1812, there appeared a long article advocating the annexation of all America, closing with the statement: "Where is it written in the book of fate that the American republic shall not stretch her limits from the capes of the Chesapeake to Nootka Sound, from the Isthmus of Panama to Hudson Bay?" The paper then editorially commended the article to its readers and followed it up with a series of historical and descriptive articles about Mexico.

The War of 1812 continued for two years. Troops were raised to invade Canada but interest in the venture was slight. Many of the militia refused to march out of American territory, as it was understood then that the militia could not be ordered to foreign soil. The expansionists could have united to declare war, but plans of expansion collapsed. The northern states opposed the annexation of Florida without Canada. The troops could never take Canada. Madison and Monroe were interested in Florida, not Canada. The British repulsed the troops from Canada. The south had no desire to acquire northern territory.

The War of 1812, in fact, was a complete failure from every angle. Our troops were defeated. General Winfield Scott declared that the army officers were "generally sunk in either sloth, ignorance, or habits of intemperate drinking," "swaggerers, dependents, decayed gentlemen utterly unfit for any military purpose whatever."

Muzzey in "The United States of America through the Civil War," Vol. I, page 253, says: "The War of 1812 was a blunder. It was unnecessary, impolitic, untimely, and rash." It was primarily the work of Henry Clay. If the United States had been in any condition to fight, we should have been of great aid to Napoleon who at that time was being defeated by Great Britain.

In the peace treaty of 1814, which brought the war to a close, the causes of the war were not mentioned. The War of 1812 was a war of paradoxes. It was waged ostensibly in defense of maritime commercial interests, but the merchant states themselves threatened to secede so as to stop it. The English Orders in Council, the alleged cause of the war, were repealed five days after war was declared and before news of its declaration reached England. The most important battle of the war, the Battle of New Orleans, was fought after the treaty of peace had been signed. The United States did not get any of the desired territory; was defeated in nearly every campaign; and the capitol was burned by the English. The land was not gained and the rights on the sea were not granted. England never yielded the right of impressment, which remained a diplomatic controversy as late as 1842.

In order to save its reputation, the Administration published an "Exposition of the Causes and Character of the War," prepared by A. J. Dallas, in which it was denied that the administration had ever tried to acquire Canada. Madison was a great scholar but not a strong executive, and it was the war hawks led by Clay who forced the war upon him and the nation.

- 20 -

BIBLIOGRAPHY

Adams, Henry—*John Randolph.*

Hocker, L. M.—"Western Land Hunger and the War of 1812; A Conjecture". *Mississippi Valley Historical Review*, Vol. X, pages 363-395.

Johnson, Allen—*Union and Democracy.* Chapter 11.

Lewis, H. J.—"A Re-analysis of the Causes of the War of 1812." *American Historical Magazine.* Vol. VI, pages 306-316, 577-584.

Muzzey, D. S.—*The United States of America Through the Civil War.* Vol. I, chapter 5.

Pratt, J. W.—*The Expansionists of 1812.*

Simons, A. M.—*Social Forces in American History.* Chapter 13.

CHAPTER IV

THE WAR WITH MEXICO

Early in the nineteenth century the people of the United States, and especially those of the south-west, became interested in that part of Mexico known as Texas. The Louisiana purchase was made in 1803. Settlers went immediately into that region along the Mississippi River. The expansionist movement then grew rapidly as we have seen, and was the major cause of the War of 1812. American settlers pushed into Mexico and soon got control of that section now known as Texas, where there were few Mexicans. These citizens of the United States went there on the assumption that Texas would some day become a part of the United States. Much of Texas was suited for the raising of cotton,—hence slavery was profitable.

In 1827 Mexico passed a law providing for the gradual abolition of slavery. The people of Texas interested in slavery, resented this, as did the pro-slavery factions in the United States. Sentiment in Texas for secession crystalized rapidly, and in 1836 Texas seceded from Mexico, later asking to be annexed to the United States. Some of the anti-slavery groups opposed this annexation which would increase the slave territory. In her constitution of 1837 Texas legalized slavery. It was not until 1845 that Texas was admitted as a state.

Polk of Tennessee, an ardent expansionist, was elected President by the Democrats in 1844. "Manifest Destiny" had then become the slogan of the Democratic party. Accordingly, President Tyler secured the annexation of Texas as a state just before his term of office closed in 1845, a few days before he was succeeded by Polk.

Texas in revolt from Mexico claimed more territory than she had possessed while a Mexican state. Her southern boundary had then been the Nueces River, but after revolting, she laid claim down to the Rio Grande River. This area between the Nueces River and the Rio Grande was sparsely settled, but its inhabitants were Mexicans and included the Mexican settlements at the mouth of the Rio Grande. Polk did not desire war but he was eager to acquire this disputed territory. He sent John Slidell, of Louisiana, as minister to Mexico to induce Mexico to accept the Rio Grande as the southern boundary of Texas rather than the Nueces River, which had been the southern boundary of Texas while a Mexican province. Slidell was also instructed to buy from Mexico the territory now comprising the states of New Mexico, California, Arizona, Utah, Nevada, and part of

- 22 -

Colorado, all of which was then a part of Mexico. Mexico, however, refused to receive Slidell or consider disposing of that territory, on the ground that the United States had annexed Texas although Mexico had not acknowledged its independence.

When Polk could not acquire this desired territory by negotiation, he ordered General Taylor to enter the Rio Grande territory. This was done on January 13, 1846. On May 9, 1846, Polk notified the cabinet of his intention to recommend a war with Mexico within a few days, by which means he hoped to take the territory he could not buy. On the night of May 9, 1846, news came to President Polk that on April 24, 1846, the American army had had a skirmish with Mexican forces. On May 11, 1846, President Polk sent a message to Congress stating Mexico had "shed American blood upon American soil. War exists, and notwithstanding all our efforts to avoid it, exists by the act of Mexico herself." And two days later, May 13, 1846, President Polk informed his cabinet that the United States must acquire New Mexico, California, and the surrounding southwest territory as a result of the war. Some of the cabinet members wanted to take all of Mexico. Secretary of State Buchanan in a public letter said: "Destiny beckons us to hold and civilize Mexico."

Americans had often tried to incite rebellions in Mexico. Many were arrested there and shot for treason. The United States, however, had never discouraged her citizens from trying to dismember Mexico.

The circumstances surrounding the outbreak of hostilities between General Taylor and the Mexicans were these: President Polk had ordered General Taylor to enter the Rio Grande River region with American troops. He was arbitrarily accepting the Rio Grande and not the Nueces River as the southern boundary of Texas. The American troops marched down to the Rio Grande opposite Matamoras, a Mexican village south of the Rio Grande. They then blockaded the town and cut off its outlet down the Rio Grande. Mexicans crossed over the Rio Grande to drive the Americans away and to make them cease their interference with this Mexican village. Some Americans were killed in the skirmish. Rhodes on page 87, Vol. I, "History of the United States," says "Mexico was actually goaded on to the war."

Mexico had notified the United States that the annexation of Texas would be treated as a cause of war. The Mexican press made threats. Yet there were so many internal quarrels in Mexico that open hostilities could have been avoided if the United States had not taken the position of supporting Texas in her claim to the Rio Grande as her southern boundary, disregarding the Nueces River as the southern boundary of Texas while a Mexican Province. Webster, Clay, Calhoun, Benton, and Tyler regarded the war as the result of poor management on the part of President Polk. The Whig party generally criticised it while the Democrats usually favored it, although, as the war continued, both groups were won over to its support. The Massachusetts legislature resolved in April, 1847, during hostilities, that the war had been "unconstitutionally commenced by the order of the President for the dismemberment of Mexico." Lincoln also criticised the war while it was in progress. He voted for a resolution offered by Mr. Ashburn in the House declaring that the war had been "unnecessarily and unconstitutionally" begun. On December 22, 1847, Mr. Lincoln offered the famous "Spot Resolution," calling upon the President to furnish Congress with information regarding the "spot" where hostilities had begun. A pamphlet was sent to Mr. Lincoln in which the author claimed that "in view of all the facts" the government of the United States had committed no aggression in Mexico. To this Mr. Lincoln replied: "It is a fact that the United States army in marching to the Rio Grande marched into a peaceful settlement, and frightened the inhabitants away from their houses and their growing crops. It is a fact that Fort Brown, opposite Matamoras, was built by that army within a Mexican cotton field, on which at the time the army reached it a young cotton crop was growing, which crop was wholly destroyed, and the field itself greatly and permanently injured by ditches, embankments, and the like." Although Lincoln voted for army supplies he always criticised the war. For this Lincoln's "patriotism" was questioned by Douglas in 1858 during the Lincoln-Douglas debates. General Grant in his Memoirs, Vol. I, page 53, said he considered the Mexican War "one of the most unjust ever waged by a stronger against a weaker nation."

The direct cost of the conflict was $100,000,000, with a death list of 1,200 men.

BIBLIOGRAPHY

Macy, Jesse—*Political Parties in the United States, 1846-1861*. Chapters 7-22.

Rhodes, James Ford—*History of the United States*. Vol. I, pages 87-92.

Stephenson, N. W.—*Texas and the Mexican War*.

Schlesinger, A. M.—*Political and Social History of the United States*. Chapter 7.

Smith, Justin H.—*The War With Mexico*. Vols. I & II.

Tarbell, Ida—*Life of Lincoln*. Vol. II, chapter 1.

Wilson, Woodrow—*Division and Reunion*, chapter 6.

CHAPTER V

THE CIVIL WAR

The Civil War was the result of a series of political crimes and blunders of which both sections of the country were equally guilty. It was not inevitable or necessary to fight in order to abolish slavery. In every other country of the world slavery had been abolished without war. The question of slavery had never been a party issue until after the Mexican War, but from then until the election of 1860 slavery was the leading political issue. During the war with Mexico, Wilmot, of Pennsylvania, offered what is known as the Wilmot Proviso, which provided that the territory acquired from Mexico should be closed to slavery. Although this bill was defeated in Congress it brought up the question of the further extension of slavery.

At the time of the Mexican War there were two national parties—the Whigs and the Democrats. These two parties embraced almost all of the people, and as both were strong in both sections of the United States, they tended to cement the union, for parties on a national basis tend to unify a nation while sectional parties lead to disunion. The anti-slavery people and the moderates gravitated towards the Whig party while the pro-slavery people gravitated towards the Democratic party.

The Whigs elected General Zachary Taylor President in 1848. Although he was a large slave holder of Louisiana, he was a moderate, and was satisfactory to all groups and sections. He had the support of Lincoln as well as of the southern Whigs. Soon after Taylor became President, Henry Clay proposed the famous Compromise of 1850, the important features of which were: admit California as a free state, organize the remainder of the territory taken from Mexico without regard to slavery, abolish the slave trade in the District of Columbia, and pass a fugitive slave law to be enforced by the federal government. This compromise, although a Whig measure, was instrumental in killing the Whig party. No party or section was satisfied with it. President Taylor opposed it but his death before its passage brought to the presidency the Vice-President, Fillmore, who allowed it to become a law without his signature. The provision that broke up the Whig party was the strict fugitive slave law, and anti-slavery Whigs repudiated their party. The idea of returning fugitive slaves was shocking to the best moral judgment of the time. The leaders of moral sentiment—ministers, poets, and reformers of every type—advised disobedience. It was a dead letter because the moral sentiment of the age was against it. On the other hand, the pro-slavery people did not like it because it was not enforced. Thus the law was treated with contempt by both parties.

The Whig party which was moderate, national, opposed to expansion, and the extension of slavery was disrupted. The Democrats carried all except four states in 1852, and remained in power until 1860, dominated by powerful pro-slavery sentiment throughout this period.

After the fall of the Whig party the Republican party was organized in 1856. It took the name "Republican" from the followers of Thomas Jefferson and claimed it was a revival of the party of Jefferson. It was the liberal party, opposed to slavery. It was organized and until after the Civil War dominated by the liberal element in the United States. The Democratic party also claimed themselves to be followers of Jefferson, which they were not, at that time, except in a very narrow legal sense. Jefferson was opposed to slavery and special privilege in every form. In 1800 he advocated state rights or a decentralized government because he believed the states were and would always be more popularly controlled than the federal government. But by 1860 that situation was reversed. The states— especially the southern states—had begun to be dominated by the privileged group, who talked in terms of state rights to perpetuate this privilege, while Jefferson talked in terms of state rights because he feared the domination of the federal government by the reactionary element. Both Lincoln and Jefferson held the same views socially. The Democratic party of the pre-Civil War period had repudiated Jefferson. But the Republican party did not become reactionary until after the Civil War.

When the Republican party was organized in 1856, it was regarded as "red," chiefly in the eyes of the south, for it was organized principally with the idea of keeping slavery out of the west. Its campaign literature in 1856 was composed largely of the anti-slavery utterances of Jefferson. To the south "Republican," "anarchy," "abolitionist," "Lincoln," "John Brown," and "Garrison" were soon to become synonymous terms. Because of this the Republican party had no following in the south even among a great many people who wished to abolish slavery. It became a sectional party, which was its fatal weakness in dealing with slavery, as compared with the former Whig party, which had had a national following. The Republican party was sectional before 1860.

Lincoln had been a Whig, and had accepted the Compromise of 1850. Although he was one of the great men of all times, he was a victim of many of the common errors of his age. Reflecting the belief of his time, he considered slavery a stable institution. His great democratic spirit lay in the fact that he expressed the ideas of the common man, and had complete faith in him. He tried to recognize and give expression to the purposes and aspirations of the masses, which made him one of the world's greatest democrats, with democracy's strengths and weaknesses. Lincoln was not a creative thinker and had few pretensions in that direction. He had no intention of abolishing slavery in the states—he simply wished to prevent it from spreading. He also held the common attitude of his age that the Negro belonged to an inferior race.

In the election of 1860 Lincoln polled only 26,430 votes in the entire south and those were from the upper section. Douglas, the moderate Democrat, received 163,525 votes in the south; Bell, of the Unionist party, received 515,973 votes in the same section, while Breckenridge, the extreme pro-slavery candidate, received 570,871 votes in the entire south. Breckenridge carried the lower south by a plurality while Lincoln carried the west and north by a plurality, and was elected president. The Douglas and Bell voters of the south were opposed to secession, but all the secession vote went to Breckenridge although not all the Breckenridge vote was for secession. A majority in the south opposed secession but the southern states fell into the hands of the secessionists by a plurality.

Why did the south secede? Lincoln was elected on a platform defying the Dred Scott decision of 1857. According to this decision the Constitution recognized slavery and therefore Congress could not prohibit it in the western territories. This could be done only by the states through their constitutions or by the federal government through a constitutional amendment. This was a great legal victory for slavery, but Lincoln defied the decision, and expected the next move on the part of pro-slavery advocates to be an attempt to legalize slavery in the northern states through a Supreme Court decision. Lincoln, when asked what he meant by saying the union could not exist half free and half slave, said that slavery would eventually have to go but it would probably last one hundred years. He did not realize that slavery was dying. This election of Lincoln on a platform defying a decision of the Supreme Court caused the lower south to secede, as a gesture to uphold the courts and the Constitution. Lincoln coerced them in order to uphold the Constitution, for he had been legally elected president and his office required his execution of federal laws. Thus, both the north and the south fought to defend the Constitution. Both felt themselves defensive—neither section understood the other—and emotionalism in the matter was so kindled that reason could not function on either side. The Civil War was a war about an abstraction—the status of slavery in the western territory—which was the real cause of the war. There were other differences between the north and the south but none of them would have resulted in war had not the slave question entered into the conflict.

By 1860 slavery in the greater part of the civilized world was a dead or a dying institution. Great Britain in 1833 abolished slavery in all her possessions. Mexico provided for the gradual abolition of slavery as early as 1827. Brazil followed in 1888 and Spain abolished slavery in Cuba in 1878. In all these cases it was done without conflict. All the northern states of the union had become free and the western states and territories were repudiating slavery as well. When California drew up her constitution and asked for admission in 1850, the clause prohibiting slavery was adopted by a unanimous vote of her constitutional convention. In the referendum held in Kansas in 1858, 11,300 out of a total vote of 13,088 were opposed to slavery. Only a few slaves had been carried there and they could never have been permanently held as slaves. New Mexico was organized as a territory in 1850 without regard to slavery and at one time as many as twenty-two slaves had been carried there. Nevada, Colorado, and Dakota were organized as territories before 1860 but had no slaves. In Missouri slavery was on the decrease, if judged by its percentage of the entire population— in 1830, 17.8% of the Missouri population were slaves; in 1840, 15.5%; in 1850, 12.8%; and in 1860, only 9.8%. Slavery would have existed in Missouri only for a few more years, for the anti-slavery population was increasing rapidly by settlers from the free states and great numbers of people from Germany who settled in the neighborhood of St. Louis, and were especially opposed to slavery.

Before 1860, slavery was non-existent in all sections of the union except the tobacco, cotton and sugar cane belts. In upholding the institution of slavery, the south was opposed to the spirit of the age. Slavery was doomed by moral and economic pressure. It was a useless procedure for the south to demand the right to carry slavery into the western territory because it was unprofitable economically and was not wanted. For the same reason it was futile for the opponents of slavery to try to prohibit by law its extension westward—the westerners had no desire or use for it. It was this contention over slavery in western territory which was the abstraction over which the Civil War was fought.

Many people before 1860, saw the folly of this controversy. Governor Robert J. Walker of Mississippi recognized that the west would never be open to slavery, as did Stanton of Tennessee and Senator Toombs of Georgia. The status of slavery in the west had been automatically settled by the laws of nature. The two sections, however, cherished perverted ideas of each other. It was reported, and actually believed, in the north, that Senator Robert Toombs, of Georgia, had boastfully declared that he would call the roll of his slaves in Massachusetts.

The following incidents given in Macy's "Political Parties in The United States," pages 209 to 211, are illustrative of the state of public excitement preceding the Civil War. In an effort to dictate the slave policy of the west, Charlie B. Lines, a deacon of a New Haven congregation, had enlisted a company of seventy-nine emigrants for the war. A meeting was held in the church shortly before their departure, for the purpose of raising funds, at which many clergymen and members of the Yale College faculty were present. The leaders of the party announced that Sharpe's rifles were lacking and that they were needed for self-defense. After an earnest address from Henry Ward Beecher, the subscription began. Professor Silliman started the subscription with one Sharpe's rifle; the pastor of the church gave the second. Fifty was the number wanted. Then Beecher announced that if twenty-five were pledged on the spot, Plymouth Church would furnish the rest. Churches in both sections had by that time become agencies for propagating hatred. Another incident is a southern one. Colonel Bufort of Alabama sold a number of his slaves valued at $20,000, and invested the money to equip a troop of three hundred soldiers to fight for southern rights in Kansas. "The day that Bufort's battalion started from Montgomery they marched to the Baptist Church. The Methodist minister solemnly invoked the divine blessing on the enterprise; the Baptist pastor gave Bufort a finely bound Bible, and said that a subscription had been raised to present each emigrant with a copy of the Holy Scripture." This battalion left for the west armed with Bibles and Sharpe's rifles. The existence of such a condition of excitement made it an easy matter to precipitate war.

In political contests the natural tendency is for persons of extreme views to gain leadership—decided and partisan convictions are easily described and understood, whereas people of moderate and discreet judgment often lack conviction themselves and so cannot very well impress their views upon the masses. Garrison's extreme abuse of the south was met there with similar other extremes. The abolitionists had great sympathy for the oppressed but great hatred for the oppressor, and regarded the slave owner as personally responsible for slavery rather than as an agent of circumstances. Perhaps if the abolitionists had directed their appeal to the moral conscience of the south, avoiding sectional and personal abuse, secession would never have taken place. The south met this abuse by demanding that all anti-slavery publications be excluded from the mails. Books, papers, and all publications suspected of containing anti-slavery propaganda were taken from the mails and publicly burned at Charleston, S. C. There were many manifestations of disregard for the sanctity of the mails. The north judged the south by these extreme actions, and the efforts of the south to suppress anti-slavery agitation resulted only in greater propaganda for the abolitionists.

The public is quick to demand war, but is not so willing to accept its hardships. During the conflict it was necessary for both the north and the south to suspend civil liberties, including freedom of the press and speech. Expressions that might weaken war morale were punished—both sections suspended the writ of habeas corpus and arbitrarily imprisoned their citizens. About 38,000 people were imprisoned in the north while the number in the south is unknown. Both sections, as in all major wars, resorted to the draft to recruit soldiers. Yet, with all these weapons at their disposal, the northern army succeeded in enlisting only about 1,325,000 of its native white population out of a total of 23,000,000. Besides approximately 1,325,000 native whites, the northern army consisted of 300,000 whites from the south, 186,000 negroes, and 500,000 foreigners. Left to the voluntary support of its citizens neither section could have carried on the war, as no major war of modern times could have been fought with that voluntary support alone. The draft acts of both sections allowed for the employment of substitutes, which, of course, was hard on the poorer classes who could not employ substitutes, but the richer classes often avoided army service by this method. It is impossible to obtain an exact figure for the number of substitutes employed, but the Secretary of War under Davis considered 50,000 a low estimate for the Confederate army in 1864. Desertion was frequent on both sides. Rhodes estimates the number of deserters in the south at 100,000 in 1864.

Much has been heard of the heroism and sacrifice displayed during the conflict, but little of the crimes committed by both sections. Only the pleasant phases of the war have survived. When Joseph Holt and Robert Dale Owen were appointed by Secretary of War Stanton to adjust claims for materials supplied to the War Department, they found fraud at every turn, and before making their final report in July, 1862, secured deductions of nearly $17,000,000 from claims amounting to $50,000,000. One claim alone was reduced $1,000,000 and another was reduced $580,000. One senator had received $10,000 for securing an order from the War Department for a client. Colonel Henry S. Olcott, who was appointed special commissioner to investigate frauds, after a thorough examination of the facts announced that from 20% to 25% of the expenditures of the Federal treasury during the Civil War was tainted with fraud, and, according to his estimate, approximately $700,000,000 was paid through fraud. (See Rhodes, Vol. V, page 220.)

In commenting upon moral conditions during the conflict, the *Springfield Republican* said editorially: "It is a sad, a shocking picture of life in Washington, which our correspondents are giving us;—a Bureau of the Treasury Department made a home of seduction and prostitution; the necessities of poor and pretty women made the means of their debauchery

- 30 -

by high government officials; members of Congress putting their mistresses into clerkships in the departments; whiskey drinking ad libitum." (See Rhodes, Vol. V, page 212.) These are some of the typical incidents of conditions in both sections, but text books in treating of this war, as of all others, present only those phases which glorify the conflict.

The cost of the Civil War, including the expenditures of both sections, pensions, destruction of property, and other indirect expenses, was $12,000,000,000. Its damage to the moral and spiritual development of the United States cannot be estimated.

BIBLIOGRAPHY

Dodd, W. E.—*The Cotton Kingdom.*

Lonn—*Desertion During the Civil War.*

Macy, Jesse—*The Anti-Slavery Crusade.*

Macy, Jesse—*Political Parties in the United States.* Chapters 7-22.

Rhodes, James Ford—*History of the United States.* Vols. I-V.

Stephenson, N. W.—*The Day of the Confederacy.*

Stephenson, N. W.—*Abraham Lincoln and the Union.*

Wood, William—*Captain of the Civil War.*

CHAPTER VI

THE WAR WITH SPAIN

For almost a century, the Spanish possession of Cuba had been regarded with disfavor by certain elements in the United States. Reasons for this attitude varied from those of acquisition on grounds of "manifest destiny," to those of the highest altruism. When the Spanish American republics won their independence during the early years of the nineteenth century, Porto Rico and Cuba remained in the possession of Spain.

Thomas Jefferson advocated the acquiring of Cuba and its annexation as a state, chiefly for fear that it would be acquired by England. Later, pro-slavery leaders wanted to take the island in order to extend slave territory, as had been done in the case of Florida and Texas. Cuba's annexation was a part of the "manifest destiny" program which was rampant in the years preceding the Civil War. Many filibustering expeditions were sent there with annexation in view. The Cubans themselves often came to the United States, became naturalized citizens of this country, and would return to Cuba with an unfriendly attitude toward Spanish authority, counting for protection on their American citizenship, in case of trouble.

There had often been spasmodic rebellions or outbreaks in Cuba before 1895. In 1868, there broke out what is known as the "Ten Years' War" which lasted until 1878, but the causes of these conflicts were never clearly understood by the participants on either side. Sugar cane was the principal source of Cuban wealth. According to the customary policy of trade barriers, Spain imposed duties on goods coming from the United States and the United States imposed high duties on Cuban sugar. These duties severely hurt Cuban economic life, and as economic depressions as well as prosperities are always attributed to the party in power regardless of the real causes, the Cubans, no exceptions to this rule, blamed the political power then in authority.

During this "Ten Years' War" many filibustering expeditions were secretly fitted out in the United States by and for the Cubans. In 1873, a ship, the *Virginius*, sailing under American colors, carrying men and supplies to the Cuban insurgents Was captured by a Spanish gunboat. The crew and passengers were given a trial which resulted in the execution of fifty-three, of whom eight claimed to be American citizens. Immediately, the war cry Went up in the United States. But, due to the wise policy of President Grant, it never gained headway.

- 32 -

Finally, in 1878, Spain agreed to forget the past, abolish slavery in Cuba, and admit delegates from Cuba to the Spanish Cortes or Parliament. The Cubans agreed, and hostilities ceased. All men in Cuba were given the ballot if they paid taxes to the amount of $25.00 annually, which still excluded the poorer classes. Of the representatives sent by the island to the Spanish Cortes or Parliament in Madrid, about one-fifth were Cuban born. This arrangement lasted as long as the economic life of Cuba was normal.

But in February, 1895, a new war for independence broke out, which was caused by a severe depression of the sugar industry resulting from the repeal in 1894 of the McKinley Tariff which had permitted the free entry of Cuban sugar into the United States, giving the Cuban sugar industry access to the United States market. The closing of the United States to Cuban sugar was a great blow to Cuba's sugar industry. Spanish authority in Cuba was held responsible, and warfare was soon established between the insurgents and Spanish authorities. A humane governor-general tried to suppress the insurrection peaceably, but without satisfactory results. Accordingly, General Weyler became Governor-General of Cuba, on February 16, 1896, and inaugurated the concentration policy, by which the inhabitants of Cuba were assembled or crowded within certain military camps, for it was impossible to distinguish the loyalists from the insurgents. As a result of this, there was great suffering and destruction.

Gomez was leader of the insurgents. He destroyed all the property he possibly could, in an endeavor to compel the United States to intervene. By attempting to destroy Spanish authority, Gomez hoped to secure the help of the United States. The insurgents were often led by Cubans who had come to America, obtained United States citizenship, and returned to the island claiming the privilege of their acquired citizenship. Between February 24, 1895, and January 22, 1897, seventy-four persons claiming to be citizens of the United States were arrested by Spanish authority, because of their activities as insurgents. But fully three-fourths of those arrested were Cubans or sons of Cubans who had been naturalized in the United States. Often, the insurgents developed their plans on American soil and secured military aid here. The federal government took precautions to prevent this, but many expeditions were made in spite of action taken to prevent them.

Our Department of State protested to Spain against the concentration policy in Cuba carried out under Governor-General Weyler, but Spain contended that her methods in suppressing rebellion in Cuba were no more severe than the methods employed by our federal government during the Civil War. Attention was called by Spain to the Sherman march through the south and to Sheridan's activities in Virginia. Spain also called attention to the Cuban Junta in New York, and claimed that the principal insurgent assistance came from American soil.

- 33 -

Congress appropriated $50,000 for the relief of Americans in Cuba, but up to the fall of 1897, only $6,000 of the $50,000 had been used, so little need was there for it.

In this war in Cuba between insurgents or rebels and Spanish authority, both sides destroyed all the property possible, although the insurgents destroyed more than the Spanish authorities. It was not nearly so destructive as our Civil War, yet what should we have thought had Spain protested against the conditions of our Civil War? Such a protest would have been treated with contempt. We had no more legal ground for questioning Spanish authority in Cuba, than Japan today would have in questioning or protesting against our policy in the Philippines. In fact, two years later, in our guerrilla warfare with the natives of the Philippines, we adopted the same concentration policy, as we shall see, against which we then protested in Cuba.

William Randolph Hearst, who was then the leader of American yellow journalism, had at this time developed his chain of newspapers from California to Boston. Early in 1897, he began advocating intervention. Appeals were made daily. Stories, crimes, and conditions were pictured in his papers and greatly exaggerated. Mr. McKinley, opposed to intervention, became President on March 4, 1897. Mark Hanna who had elected Mr. McKinley President, now wished to be compensated by an appointment to the United States Senate from Ohio. To create a vacancy in the Senate, Mr. McKinley appointed as his Secretary of State Mr. John Sherman who was then Senator from Ohio, and Mr. Hanna was appointed by the Governor of Ohio to the United States Senate. Mr. McKinley's appointment of John Sherman as Secretary of State was a great blunder. Mr. Sherman was then very old and rapidly declining. His work was left in the hands of his assistants in the Department of State.

United States citizens owned wealth in Cuba, to the amount of $50,000,000 and our commerce with Cuba amounted to $100,000,000 annually. These interests, of course, demanded intervention. Our Department of State in its correspondence with Spain estimated that $16,000,000 worth of American property had been destroyed in Cuba at the close of 1897, for which property Spain was held responsible. This was a greatly exaggerated figure, for at the close of the war a claims commission was created by Congress to investigate those claims, and this commission recognized as valid claims amounting to only about $362,252.

In October, 1897, Spain recalled Governor-General Weyler, and appointed in his place Blanco. The concentration order was revoked. Spain offered the natives a larger share of self-government, with their own constitution and legislature. Autonomy was granted. If it had been offered

- 34 -

three years before, this would, no doubt, have solved the problem. But now it was difficult to reconcile the two factions in Cuba. The native Spaniards in Cuba opposed home rule, as it would give the Cubans too much power. The Cubans wanted independence, and were unwilling to co-operate with the Spaniards in home rule. A Cuban parliament was called on May 4, 1898.

The Hearst newspapers were then demanding intervention on the part of the United States and moulding public opinion in that direction. Although the election of 1896 was over, and it had settled the issue of free silver, yet other social elements had entered American politics through the election and campaign of 1896, and it was in the interests of some people to make use of a "vigorous foreign policy" to keep public attention away from the new issues. This is an old device for obliterating home issues or differences. Lincoln had been advised to precipitate the United States into a foreign war as a means of preventing the Civil War.

On February 9, 1898, the *New York Journal*, a strong advocate of intervention, violated the sanctity of the United States mails by securing through criminal methods a private letter written by Lome, the Spanish minister at Washington, to a friend. In this letter Lome severely criticised McKinley, and spoke of him with contempt. This letter was published by the *New York Journal*. It excited public opinion, and was, of course, made use of by the jingo press. However, it had nothing to do with the case, for a foreign minister naturally has a perfect legal and moral right to have any opinion of the President or any other public official he likes, and to express it privately to a friend. The actual crime was in stealing the letter from the United States mails, but that action was never investigated or punished by the United States, which should have been done. Lome's criticism of McKinley may have been unjust, but he had a personal right to it.

In the midst of the great excitement created by the Lome letter, another incident took place of advantage to the war party. On January 24, 1898, the *Maine* was ordered to Cuba on a "friendly visit." This trip was accepted officially as a complimentary visit, but privately both Spain and the United States regarding it in the opposite light. After being in Havana harbor for three weeks, the *Maine* was blown up on February 15, 1898. "Remember the Maine" now became the slogan of the war party. Spain denied any connection with its destruction, and no one now believes it was blown up by Spain. The actual cause of the explosion is not known, but it is now believed to have been done by the rebels in Cuba for the purpose of securing the intervention of the United States. It may have been an accident with which Spain could in no way be connected, yet, at the time, in the eyes of the public, Spain was held responsible.

McKinley, during this period, opposed intervention, but the war party, supported by the Hearst papers, was growing rapidly. Our able minister in Spain, General Woodford, was also opposed to our intervention. Congress, however, held the opposite attitude. A senator said to Assistant Secretary of State Day: "Day, doesn't your President know where the war-declaring power is lodged? Tell him that if he doesn't do something, Congress will exercise the power." Congressman Boutelle, who was opposed to the war, says that forty or fifty Republican members of Congress held a caucus and sent a committee to the President stating that unless he asked for a declaration of war, they would propose a resolution for war and carry it through. Secretary of War Alger, who was a notorious spoilsman, said to a senator: "I want you to advise the President to declare war. He is making a great mistake. He is in danger of ruining himself and the Republican party by standing in the way of the people's wishes. Congress will declare war in spite of him. He'll get run over and the party with him." Rhodes, in "McKinley and Roosevelt Administrations," on page 64, says: "McKinley feared a rupture in his own party, and on account of that fear, had not the nerve and power to resist the pressure for war. We may rest assured that if Mark Hanna had been President, there would have been no war with Spain."

McKinley was opposed to the war up to the last of March, 1898. Only two members of his cabinet were in favor of war. Also, the Vice-President was against it, as was Mark Hanna, the Speaker of the House, and nearly all the leading Republicans of the Senate.

On March 29, 1898, McKinley sent his ultimatum to Spain demanding the complete abandonment of the concentration policy, the granting of an armistice to Cuba, and the opening of peace negotiations through himself with the insurgents. Spain replied granting the complete abandonment of the concentration policy and did not refuse to grant the armistice, but told our minister, General Woodford, that she would gladly grant it, if the Cubans, who were the resistors, asked for it, for Spain could not first offer it. Our minister at Madrid then cabled McKinley that the Spanish government and people wished to settle the difficulty without war, and that in a few months' time, he would "get peace in Cuba, with justice to Cuba and protection to our great American interests."

Let us say, for example, that Japan had sent an ultimatum to McKinley during the Philippine insurrection, demanding that he change his policy of coercion and grant an armistice to the Philippines. Such a demand would have been treated with contempt, yet that is what we demanded of Spain.

On April 6, 1898, the representatives of Great Britain, Germany, France, Austria, Russia, and Italy made an appeal to McKinley to continue peaceful negotiations. The Pope also intervened for peace. He asked the Queen of Spain to comply fully with our ultimatum. Accordingly, on April 10, McKinley was notified by the Foreign Office at Madrid, that Spain would grant the armistice. But on the following day, Monday, April 11, 1898, McKinley appeared before Congress and asked for a declaration of war against Spain, without informing them of the latest concessions made by Spain. It is impossible to explain McKinley's action. Through the efforts of Minister Woodford, at Madrid, and others, a diplomatic victory had been won only to be thrown away by McKinley and Congress. The Spanish minister at Washington was notified that the President in his message to Congress on April 11, would explain the concession made by Spain, but this was not done—a reference only was made to it in his war message.

War was declared on April 18 by a vote of 324 to 19 in the House, and 67 to 21 in the Senate. On March 31, 1898, Woodford had cabled to McKinley: "I believe the ministry are ready to go as far and as fast as they can and still save the dynasty here in Spain. They know that Cuba is lost. Public opinion in Spain has moved steadily towards peace." Then on April 3, 1898, Woodford sent this message to President McKinley: "The Spanish Minister for Foreign Affairs assures me that Spain will go as far and as fast as she can. I know that the Queen and her present ministry sincerely desire peace, and that the Spanish people desire peace, and if you can still give me time and reasonable liberty of action, I am sure that before next October 1st, I will get peace in Cuba." Again on April 10, the day before our declaration of war, Woodford notified our Department of State that before August 1, he could secure autonomy for Cuba, or a recognition of its independence by Spain or a cession of the island to the United States. He then added: "I hope that nothing will be done to humiliate Spain, as I am satisfied the present government is going, and is loyally ready to go, as fast and as far as it can." It was an open secret that Spain would give up or sell Cuba as soon as she could.

One cannot read the Woodford dispatches and fail to see that the Spanish-American War was thrust upon Spain by our jingo press. President McKinley over-estimated its strength and lost his nerve, fearing the disruption of his party. Spain was not surprised but "stunned" when the United States declared war, a war which cannot be defended on any grounds. Cuba was Spanish territory and we had no more legal right to intervene than Spain, for example, had a right to demand that the United States change her methods of government in Alaska. Morally, the war was indefensible, for Spain was conceding and was ready to go to any extent to avoid war, even to the point of granting independence to Cuba. This conflict with Spain cost $300,000,000, not including the indirect expenses.

The most important result of the war was our acquisition of the Philippine Islands. In February, 1898, about two months before war was declared, Admiral Dewey of the American fleet was ordered to Hongkong, China, and instructed to be prepared to begin operations against the Philippines in case of a declaration of war. Until after the battle of Manila, the American people had practically never heard of the Philippine Islands. These islands were taken, however, and at the peace conference, Mr. McKinley instructed our commissioners not to be satisfied with anything less than the entire group of islands because of the "commercial opportunity,"—they were secured as a trading base in the Orient. At that time, it seemed that China would be dismembered by the European powers and that unless we secured the Philippines, the United States would have no share in the Orient. This was our first step in a policy of imperialism, clothed in mild terms.

For three years after our capture of these islands, the natives put up a guerrilla warfare to resist the United States forces. During this period, the American army resorted to every description of barbaric torture. Among other measures, the policy of concentrating the inhabitants in camps was resorted to, which was the same policy we objected to the use of by Spain in Cuba. Prisoners of war were executed in retaliation for crimes of which they knew nothing. One of our notorious army officers known as "Hell-Roaring" Jake Smith commanded that every building in a certain area be burned and every native over ten years of age be slain.

These three years of guerrilla warfare cost the United States $170,000,000. All of this cost and cruelty, aside from being unjust, was unnecessary, for the natives of the Philippines were willing to co-operate with the United States to develop their civilization by peaceful methods. The resistance was caused by the presence of United States soldiers in the islands.

BIBLIOGRAPHY

Beard, Charles A.—*Contemporary American History*. Chapter 8.

Chadwick, F. E.—*Relations of United States and Spain*.

Latane, J. H.—*America as a World Power*. Chapters 1-5.

Powers, H. H.—*America Among the Nations*.

Rhodes, James Ford—*The McKinley and Roosevelt Administrations*. Chapters 3, 4, 5.

Schlesinger, A. M.—*Political and Social History of the United States*. Chapters 14 and 15.

Storey, M.—*The Conquest of the Philippines*.

CHAPTER VII

THE WORLD WAR

We shall not undertake a long discussion of the causes of the World War but simply examine the reasons for the participation in it of the United States on the side of the Allies. For the first time in history the generation living through a great war has been able to ascertain the facts regarding its origin. These facts, however, have not yet become the common property of the great masses, although they are gradually becoming evident to everybody. A great many people are still influenced by the passions and hatreds aroused by the conflict.

Briefly stated, the causes of the conflict were trade rivalry between Great Britain and Germany, the scramble for territory especially in Africa, the conflict between Russia and Germany for the domination of the Balkan Peninsula, and the old inherited animosity between France and Germany. The accusation of "sole" guilt against Germany is held no longer by persons who have studied the facts, although there still are and will no doubt always be differences of opinion about minor points. The immediate occasion for the opening of hostilities in 1914 was the murder of Archduke Ferdinand, the heir to the throne of Austria-Hungary. This murder took place while he was in Bosnia. The crime was committed by representatives of a Pan-Slavic organization working hand in hand with the Serbian government with a view to annexing Bosnia to Serbia.

Up to the nineteenth century, the Balkan Peninsula was owned by Turkey, but the last century has witnessed the gradual break-up of European Turkey on the Balkan Peninsula. In connection with this disintegration, Russia tried to gain territory at the expense of Turkey. Austria-Hungary also tried to penetrate the same area. A conflict was the inevitable consequence. This Balkan problem had been a source of trouble in Europe for a century. The people of Serbia were Slavs and looked to Russia for support,—in fact, Serbia was practically governed by Russian diplomacy. Austria-Hungary looked to Germany for support. In 1908, Bosnia, which was then a Turkish province but had been administered by Austria-Hungary since 1878, was annexed by Austria-Hungary. This act offended Serbia, who wished to annex it as part of the Pan-Slavic dream for the domination by Russia of Bosnia, Serbia, and the remainder of the Balkans. This annexation by Austria-Hungary defeated the Pan-Slavic dream and was a victory for Pan-Germany. Feeling became more and more acute when in 1914 the Archduke Ferdinand was killed. The incident was applauded by Serbia, and conflict followed. The details of events in 1914 are too complicated to go into for our brief space, but popular accounts reaching the United States were from Allied sources and were correspondingly biased.

In 1914 all Europe was divided into two great military camps—the Allied and the Central Powers. The following is the size of the principal armies of Europe in 1914: Germany, 806,000; Austria, 370,000; Italy, 305,000; France, 818,000; Russia, 1,284,000; Belgium, 280,000. All Europe was equipped as a military machine, and the murder in 1914 simply put the machinery in motion. It was an absurd fallacy to think that Germany was the only armed nation at the time, and to believe that Great Britain entered the conflict to defend Belgium is equally absurd. As early as 1911, Great Britain had made plans with France for marching an army through Belgium to Germany in the event of war with Germany. Belgium was regarded as part of the Allied powers. Great Britain has officially acknowledged to be false her ostensible reason for entering the war—the protection of Belgium. Her reason was the struggle between rival imperialisms, which secret treaties later exposed show clearly.

However, we are concerned here only with why the United States entered the war. The three outstanding causes were interference with neutral trade, economic ties with the Allies, and Allied propaganda in the United States. These causes overlap in such a way as to make it impossible to discuss them separately.

Soon after war was declared in 1914, Great Britain placed mines in the North Sea and with the aid of her navy blockaded Germany and the adjacent neutral portions of North Europe. As a result, all goods going in that direction were captured. The United States protested, but Great Britain refused to yield the point, claiming it to be a military necessity albeit illegal from the point of view of international law. Great Britain blockaded Germany by mines, and cut off all foreign trade with Germany and neutral ports near Germany to prevent the entrance of goods into Germany. Germany retaliated in February, 1915, by employing the submarine to blockade Great Britain. One policy was as legal as the other. Mr. Wilson protested, but neither side yielded. In no case in history has a nation at war observed the established rules if the rules conflict with military expediency. The United States has been no exception to this procedure. Since the object of warfare is the physical destruction of an opponent, once you justify the war you must justify any means employed to gain the victory. In protesting to Germany, we argued that the submarines could not warn ships to take off passengers before they were sunk, but neither could the mines planted by Great Britain. American ships kept out of the mine zones but disregarded the submarine zones for reasons we shall later explain. The *Lusitania*, a British ship, was sunk by a submarine on May 7, 1915. One hundred and fourteen Americans lost their lives. We immediately protested. But the facts have shown that the *Lusitania* carried a large quantity of munitions of war. At the time the boat was sunk a United States senator asked the Treasury Department for the bill of lading. He was told it had been turned over to the State Department. When the senator asked the State Department for a copy of the bill of lading in order to see what was on board, the State Department refused to disclose the contents, on the grounds that it was to be kept for diplomatic correspondence. It was not known till after the war was over what had actually been on board the ship. Since then it has been officially stated by the collector of customs then at New York that the *Lusitania* carried munitions of war. Besides, Germany had warned the passengers before getting on board that in all probability the ship would be sunk. This notice was officially published in the New York papers before the ship sailed. There is no question but that the passengers had been given due warning. Whether the sinking was legal or not depends upon the point of view. According to Germany, she did more than the law required by her warning before the ship left harbor, which is rather better than being warned a few minutes before being sunk in mid-ocean.

The British seized and searched the mails. United States officials below the rank of minister were searched by the British while traveling to and from the continent. Before the close of 1914, thirty-one cargoes of copper valued at $5,500,000 had been captured by Great Britain, but the United States owners were compensated. Their seizure, however, was illegal. Early in 1916, Germany agreed to give up the use of the submarine, but on condition that the United States make Great Britain obey international law. We could not force Great Britain to abide by international law, and consequently Germany resumed her submarine warfare in 1917, which was our official reason for entering the war. But this was only our legal excuse. The effective causes were our economic ties with the Allies, and Allied propaganda in the United States. We will examine these causes more carefully.

Modern warfare is a conflict of economic resources as well as armies. The British navy cut off all economic intercourse between Germany and the United States. In this way, the economic resources of the United States were in the hands of the Allies. American agriculture, credit, and industry soon became indispensable to the Allied cause. In 1915 an Anglo-French mission came to New York and secured a loan of $500,000,000. This money was left with various banks in New York for the purpose of buying supplies from America. The Allied governments continued to borrow in

Wall Street, and these banks loaned England and France money with which to buy materials. Soon the House of Morgan became the purchasing agent of the Allies. The Morgan firm selected Edward R. Stetinius, President of the Diamond Match Company, as the purchasing agent. Mr. Stetinius selected one hundred and seventy-five men to assist him in the task. They were soon purchasing supplies for the Allies at the rate of $10,000,000 a day. By September, 1917, the Morgan firm had purchased $3,000,000,000 in merchandise and munitions for the Allies in addition to the selling of Allied bonds. The day the United States declared war against Germany the British government's bank account with Morgan was heavily overdrawn.

When Kitchener became Minister of War in Great Britain in 1915 one of his first acts was to cable Charles M. Schwab of the Bethlehem Steel Company to come to England immediately. Schwab went and agreed to sell all the output of the Bethlehem Steel Company to the British government. In less than two years, he shipped about $300,000,000 worth of war material to England. Twenty submarines were built and sent in parts to Canada where they were assembled and sent across to England. This was done a year before the German submarine *Deutschland* came to the United States and was advertised as the first to cross the Atlantic. (See John Moody, "Masters of Capital," pages 162-172.)

American industry had become one with the Allies. Our greatest banking and industrial institutions had become dependent upon an Allied victory and an Allied victory was dependent upon them. American industry became pro-Ally because the British blockade cut off our trade with Germany. German and Austrian agents such as Dumba, Karl Boy-Ed and Franz von Papen were expelled from the country because of their un-neutral activities on behalf of the Central Powers.

"Patriotic" societies such as "The Navy League," "The American Defense Society," and the "National Security League" were all tied up financially with munition plants. These societies were propaganda bureaus for "preparedness" and later for our entrance into the conflict. The nineteen men who founded the Navy League had among their number representatives of the three manufacturers of armor plate in America,—the Midvale, Bethlehem, and Carnegie Companies. The Navy League was in practice the propaganda bureau of the three companies working together to sell armor plate.

Modern warfare has become even more than a conflict of armies and of economic resources. Propaganda to secure popular support, has become more and more necessary. Both sides in the European conflict made great efforts to present their propaganda before America, but the Central Powers failed primarily because of the British blockade. The Allies, on their side, had the co-operation of American business, and easily accomplished their purpose. Professor Hayes in his "Brief History of the Great War" says: "The British resorted to every known device of propaganda from employing secret service agents in New York to maintaining at Washington the great journalist, Lord Northcliffe, with a host of assistants, as a publicity director." These propagandists had the co-operation of the bankers who had made loans to the Allies or had acted as purchasing agents. All this happened in 1916, but the American people never knew the source of their "war news" until the conflict was over. Mr. Rathom, of the Providence *Journal*, of Providence, R.I., was notorious for his accounts of German "crimes." The Boston *Herald* of December 30, 1923, in an editorial comment, says: "It is, of course, true, as most well informed people now understand, that the Rathom disclosures which made the Providence *Journal* famous during the war were fiction—but Rathom did this for the praiseworthy purpose of arousing his countrymen to a war fury. He took one of the practical ways of doing so." Captain Ferdinand Tuohy of the British Secret Service in "The Secret Corps" says: "All the trickery and subterfuge and war-wisdom of the ages brought up-to-date, intensified and harnessed to every modern invention and device, ... a Machiavelli, a Talleyrand or some other master schemer of the ages come back to earth, would have thrilled at the amazing cunning and corruption of it all." The Belgium authorities themselves have denied the truth of the crimes given out in the Bryce Report. Mr. Lloyd George has stated in print that careful investigations disclosed no case of Belgian children with hands cut off. Yet these are some of the crimes with which the American public were fed during 1916, 1917 and 1918. The peoples of the Central Powers were, of course, furnished similar crimes attributed to the Allies. There were many crimes committed as in all wars, but every nation, including the United States, was guilty of them.

It is not easy to explain the attitudes of many prominent officials of the United States during the years preceding our entrance into the war. Ambassador Walter H. Page, our representative in London, was guilty of direct disloyalty to the American Government and people. When President Wilson protested to the British Government against her disregard of neutral rights Mr. Page did not give the messages to Sir Edward Grey of the British Foreign Office. He would read them to him and would then ask Grey to co-operate with him in making a reply to the United States. Sir Edward Grey says in his memoirs: "Page came to see me at the foreign office one day and produced a long dispatch from Washington contesting our claims to act as we were doing in stopping contraband in going to neutral ports. 'I am instructed' he said 'to read this dispatch to you.' He read and I listened. He then said 'I have now read the dispatch but I do not agree with it. Let us consider how it should be answered.'" In all diplomacy there is no other example of such a procedure. Page was determined upon our entrance from the very beginning of the war. Many of our representatives at the principal courts of Europe were connected with the Allies personally through business or banking interests in this country.

Mr. Wilson himself was pro-British in scholarship. He was a great admirer of the cabinet-parliamentary form of government used in England. All his heroes in political science were English authorities. Mr. Wilson's former attorney-general, Thomas W. Gregory, says in a letter to the New York *Times* of February 9, 1925, that Wilson was "by inheritance, tradition, and reasoning at all times the friend of the Allies." Mr. Tumulty also now says Mr. Wilson was never neutral.

President Wilson had become converted to the idea of intervention by the spring of 1916. Sir Edward Grey says in his memoirs that Colonel House assured him in February, 1916, that Wilson would do his best to bring the United States to the aid of the Allies. In April, 1916, the President consulted Champ Clark, Speaker of the House; Claude Kitchen, Democratic Leader; H. D. Flood, Chairman of the Foreign Relations Committee; and other Democratic leaders regarding their willingness to bring the United States into the war on the Allied side. This is known as the famous "Sunrise Conference." They refused, and Mr. Wilson allowed his party to use as the 1916 slogan, "He kept us out of war." At the time he was afraid to advocate intervention for fear of splitting his party. There were demands on the part of certain political leaders and the press for immediate intervention but these demands were not representative of public opinion at the time. Ambassador Page brought his influence to bear on preventing the Allies from considering German proposals for peace offered in 1916 and 1917.

Allied propaganda represented Germany as lustful for world dominion. Careful examination now shows that there was no such policy except that which is common to all powers. This was part of the false propaganda spread in the United States to inflame public opinion and make our entrance "defensive." Both sides resorted to trickery of every description. Much stir was created by the Zimmermann note published in March, 1917. It was a proposal by Germany to Mexico to enter on the side of Germany should the United States join the Allies, with a view to recovering New Mexico and the surrounding territory taken by the United States from Mexico in 1848. But this was exactly what the Allies had done, when they persuaded Japan to enter in order to capture the German sphere of influence in Shantung, China. It is obvious that every nation at war will try to weaken its opponent. We encouraged the Latin American republics to declare war on Germany, which was no more than Germany did in encouraging Mexico to declare war on the United States, should we declare war on Germany. This note was distorted and reported in 1917 in a manner to give the impression that Germany was actively trying to create trouble for the United States even in peace. The fact remains that the Zimmermann proposal was not to apply unless we entered the war against Germany, when it would be a legitimate defensive measure for Germany to secure the aid of Mexico.

Brigadier General J. C. Charteris, Chief of Intelligence of the British Army during the war, stated boastfully, in New York, in an address in the fall of 1925, before the National Arts Club, that he had invented the report that Germany was boiling down the bodies of her dead soldiers to be used as fertilizer. He made the statement under the impression that no reporters were present. The Richmond *Times-Dispatch*, on December 6, 1925, said editorially:

"Not the least of the horrors of modern warfare is the propaganda bureau which is an important item in the military establishment of every nation. Neither is it the least of the many encouraging signs which each year add to the probability of eventual peace on earth.

"The famous cadaver story which aroused hatred against the German to the boiling point in this and other allied nations during the war has been denounced as a lie in the British House of Commons. Months ago, the world learned the details of how this lie was planned and broadcasted by the efficient officer in the British intelligence service. Now we are told that 'imbued with the spirit of the Locarno pact,' Sir Austen Chamberlain rose in the House, said that the German Chancellor had denied the truth of the story and that the denial had been accepted by the British government.

"A few years ago, the story of how the Kaiser was reducing human corpses to fat, aroused the citizens of this and other enlightened nations to a fury of hatred. Normally sane men doubled their fists and rushed off to the nearest recruiting sergeant. Now they are being told, in effect, that they were dupes and fools; that their own officers deliberately goaded them to the desired boiling point, using an infamous lie to arouse them, just as a grown bully whispers to one little boy that another little boy said he could lick him.

"The encouraging sign found in this revolting admission of how modern war is waged is the natural inference that the modern man is not overeager to throw himself at his brother's throat at the simple word of command. His passions must be played upon, so the propaganda bureau has taken its place as one of the chief weapons.

"In the next war, the propaganda must be more subtle and clever than the best the World War produced. These frank admissions of wholesale lying on the part of trusted governments in the last war will not soon be forgotten."

After the United States entered the war in April, 1917, we immediately created a government propaganda bureau, which was known as "The Committee on Public Information," with George Creel as chairman. Since the war, Mr. Creel has given us an account of the propaganda activities in his book—"How We Advertised America." No effort was made to present the truth. Allied propaganda was accepted and to it we added ours. This "Committee on Public Information" issued 75,099,023 pamphlets and books to encourage the public "morale." They hired the services of 75,000 speakers who operated in 5,200 communities. Altogether, about 755,190 speeches were made by these people known as the "Four Minute Men." Exhibits were given at fairs, and war films were prepared for the cinema, from which the Committee on Public Information received a royalty. A total of 1,438 drawings were employed to arouse popular hatred. An official daily newspaper was issued which had a circulation of 100,000 copies. A propaganda bureau was established by the United States, in the capitals of every nation in the world except those of the Central Powers. The total expenditure by the United States for propaganda was $6,738,223. (See George Creel, "How We Advertised America," Chapter I.) This was the greatest fraud ever sold to the public in the name of patriotism and religion.

The Espionage Act was passed making it illegal to spread "false" reports that would hinder recruiting. Every report was false which did not harmonize with the propaganda released by this Committee on Public Information. The best we can now say for Mr. Wilson and the American public is that they were the victims of Allied propaganda, and contributed to the wrecking of civilization.

BIBLIOGRAPHY

Beard, Charles A.—*Cross Currents in Europe Today.*

Barnes, Harry E.—*The Genesis of the World War.*

Creel, George—*How We Advertised America.*

Chafee, Zechariah—*Freedom of Speech.*

Fay, A. S.—*Origin of the World War.*

Flick, A. C.—*Modern World History.* Chapter 34.

Grattan, C. H.—*Why We Fought.*

Lasswell, H. D.—*Propaganda Technique in the World War.*

Moody, John—*Masters of Capital*. Chapter 9.

Nock, A. J.—*The Myth of a Guilty Nation*.

www.ingramcontent.com/pod-product-compliance
Ingram Content Group UK Ltd.
Pitfield, Milton Keynes, MK11 3LW, UK
UKHW031846210225
455402UK00004B/330